T0130395

An Angel

ON MY SHOULDER

LORI SZEPELAK

Copyright © 2023 Lori Szepelak.

All rights reserved. No part of this book may be used or reproduced by any means, graphic, electronic, or mechanical, including photocopying, recording, taping or by any information storage retrieval system without the written permission of the author except in the case of brief quotations embodied in critical articles and reviews.

Balboa Press books may be ordered through booksellers or by contacting:

Balboa Press
A Division of Hay House
1663 Liberty Drive
Bloomington, IN 47403
www.balboapress.com
844-682-1282

Because of the dynamic nature of the Internet, any web addresses or links contained in this book may have changed since publication and may no longer be valid. The views expressed in this work are solely those of the author and do not necessarily reflect the views of the publisher, and the publisher hereby disclaims any responsibility for them.

Any people depicted in stock imagery provided by Getty Images are models, and such images are being used for illustrative purposes only. Certain stock imagery © Getty Images.

Original book design by Robin Brooks, The Beauty of Books, 2010
Loriszepelak.com

ISBN: 979-8-7652-4284-1 (sc)
ISBN: 979-8-7652-4283-4 (e)

Library of Congress Control Number: 2023910253

Print information available on the last page.

Balboa Press rev. date: 06/14/2023

Also by Lori Szepelak

Floors of the Forest

Visits with Mom: A Journey Through Time and Beyond

Dedicated to my parents, Thelma and Francis
Josephson, and to my guardian angels.

Contents

Preface

When I first self published *An Angel on My Shoulder* in 2010, I wondered if I had understood the angelic messages I had received more than a year earlier.

On December 16, 2010, I would be picking up my first 300 copies at the local print shop and was excited to slip a press release in a few to send to the local media outlets in western Massachusetts.

Just a few days earlier, on Dec. 12, I was forever convinced that *An Angel on My Shoulder* was indeed meant to be birthed into the world.

As I sat at my desk on Dec. 12 and started writing a press release - I put a simple headline in bold at the top: "Southampton woman self publishes book on guardian angels," and spent some time detailing what I thought readers should know about angels and loved ones who have passed.

At that moment in time, I was still questioning whether I had followed the messages I had received from angel encounters since my mom's passing. While I was excited to hold the first copies in my hands, a sense of trepidation crept in - I wondered if this book is what the angelic realm wanted at this time on Mother Earth.

Once I finished the press release, I went back to the bold headline and having worked in the newspaper field for many years, I knew that was a boring headline.

I stared at the headline and reassured myself that I could think of something more creative if I just took a few moments to think about it. After a couple of minutes in contemplation, I felt a bit frustrated with myself, and then after 10 minutes, a sadness engulfed my being.

As I sat at my desk, I looked up toward my angels and acknowledged how far we had come since the first angel messages were relayed to me. I said I felt like I was letting them down at this point because I couldn't think of a good headline for the press release. As I glanced away from the release, I started moving papers on the other side of my desk. Within 30 seconds of glancing away, I felt this sense to look back at my computer screen.

As I turned back toward my screen, the press release was still there but the headline was noticeably longer than I had written.

I did a double take as I read the headline now in front of me - "Southampton woman self publishes book on guardian angels - because her angels asked her to."

I sat stunned and started crying. I looked up at my angels once more and said, "Thank you, thank you, thank you." I also noted to my angels - "Now that will get an editor's attention!"

What I believe in that moment was my angels knew I needed to be confident when I started my lectures in January 2011, and with that simple addition to my headline, my confidence has never wavered.

What I know is that *An Angel on My Shoulder* has its purpose to lift up others who have lost loved ones and want to know they are ok on the other side.

I give gratitude before every lecture for the opportunity to share these messages with others and feel blessed that the angelic realm chose me to be a messenger.

Over the years I have been graced with many angel encounters - in large part - after lectures when someone will share a special moment that they made a connection - or saw an angel themselves.

One of the most memorable and profound times I experienced following a lecture at a public library in Williamstown, Mass., was when a woman shared what she saw as I spoke. She told me she was stunned when she saw a beautiful large angel hovering to my right as I lectured. The woman said the angel looked lovingly at me and would nod her head in agreement as I spoke. She chose not to share those comments with the audience during the question-and-answer segment, however, and waited until everyone had left the book signing - noting she felt it was a personal moment that should be shared in beautiful stillness. I am forever grateful to her for sharing that encounter with me which I in turn have shared at countless lectures.

Another message I received repeatedly from lecture attendees was "maybe you are suppose to write three books." I heard that message from so many in the early years and always acknowledged the message but in truth never believed it would be true.

In 2010 when I was finished this book, I only believed in my heart that *An Angel on My Shoulder* would be the only book I would write.

Of course, the angels and the universe knew what was to come. In the ensuing years I published my second book, *Floors of the Forest*, in 2013, and the third, *Visits with Mom: A Journey Through Time and Beyond*, came to fruition in 2018. Each book is a continuation of the spiritual lessons I've learned over the years and additional messages that the angelic realm - and my mom - wanted to share with the world. Both books were published by Balboa Press.

Now in 2023, I feel I have come full circle. I have felt a deep need to publish *An Angel on My Shoulder* with Balboa Press, featuring this preface with a few updates on the original text.

I have come to learn so many more truths about the universe that I could never have learned without my mom's intervention and the angels all those years ago. I have read countless books and continued to receive messages from the other side - especially when I least expect them - and now my hope is this book reaches so many more people - especially in light of the COVID pandemic when millions of families suffered the loss of a loved one.

My prayer is for people who are grieving and in need of knowing that their loved one is ok and at peace - that *An Angel on My Shoulder* lifts their heart and shows them what is possible when reaching out to the love in the universe that surrounds us.

Also … a note on the book cover …

As I started lecturing in 2011, I would talk about the cover photo and the images I could see of my mom and dad in the cloud formations. I explained I had taken a photo of my husband kayaking while we were on vacation and at that particular moment in time, I was getting tired and wanted to turn back.

While I was talking to my parents, I said, "Mom, you can't help me with this request. I need Dad's strength to get back to shore."

My dad was a laborer all his life and had such large, strong hands that when he put his arms around me - I knew I was safe and I knew I was loved. I looked up at Dad and said, "Please give me the strength I need to paddle back to shore."

I took a few more photos of my husband and then called out to him to say it was time to head back to the resort.

That night as I was looking at all of the photos I had taken on that kayaking adventure, I noticed the image of my mom and a darkness that was attached to a pink image. When I zoomed in on the pink aura I saw my dad's face. I realized in that moment that both my mom and dad wanted me to know they heard me and were right there in a beautiful photo I could treasure.

As I shared this story at lectures, attendees over time would say, "What about the angel?"

I have to be honest - I didn't see her immediately - yet she is clearly above my mom and dad's images. Since I had been so focused on my mom and dad, I totally missed the beautiful white angel that also graced the photo I had taken.

One of the many lessons I've learned is that our loved ones who have passed - and our angels - can be right in front of our eyes - however, are we in so much of a rush that we don't take the time to study our photos to see if we have a beautiful gift of love waiting for us.

I also encourage those who find a beautiful gift of love - in whatever form it takes - to take a photo if possible, print it out and frame it - and share the significance of the photo with as many people as possible.

What I have learned from the angelic realm is we can all be messengers of the light - and can uplift people who may be grieving - by sharing a simple message of love from a photograph.

I am grateful for every opportunity I have to share these messages of love from the other side - and feel blessed when I receive an email from someone who either read this book and/or attended a lecture and then had their prayer answered with a treasured gift of love.

As I look back - and now forward - I am thankful for the many blessings I have received and hope in the years to come that the simple, beautiful messages in this book continue to resonate with the hearts of those around the planet.

Blessings always ...

Acknowledgments

Thank you to Wendy Birchall, an angel reader, who opened up the world of guardian angels to me.

Also, thank you to George O'Brien, a wonderful friend and confidant, who graciously agreed to review my original book, providing inspirational and creative suggestions.

Much love to my husband Bruce for all his ongoing support on this journey of mine, as well as to my family and friends who allowed me to use their photo images and share them with others.

I would also like to thank Robin Brooks of The Beauty of Books for her patience as she helped me blend my words and photographs into my beautifully designed original book in 2010.

Also, thank you to Ruth Elkin and Francie King for their copywriting assistance in 2010.

My gratitude extends to the spiritual realm, where I thank my heavenly Father, my own guardian angels, and my mom, Thelma, and dad, Francis, for ensuring that this book was published.

I also want to thank the team at Balboa Press for working with me on this second edition of *An Angel on My Shoulder*.

I give gratitude to the universe for leading me to this point in time where my hope is that countless people around Mother Earth will be touched by the messages from the angelic realm and that their hearts will be lifted.

Introduction

"Pull the plug," she scratched out on a plain white piece of paper. My heart sank.

It was part of our last conversation with my mother on June 8, 2008, in the intensive care unit of a small community hospital in western Massachusetts. As my sister Bonnie and I stood over her, Mom made it clear, in one of her last bursts of strength, that she had had enough. She didn't want to fight anymore.

Less than 24 hours later, she passed away. She was 93.

Two weeks earlier Mom had been fine, reading a book a day and doing crossword puzzles to keep her mind sharp. She loved life and everyone around her, from her family and friends to her caregivers in the nursing home where she lived.

But everything changed one morning. She took a medication that lodged in her throat, leading to aspiration pneumonia. Because of complications arising from this, she spent her last two weeks in and out of consciousness at the local hospital. Physicians gave her one last option, to have a tracheotomy. Not wishing to let go of life, Mom agreed to the procedure, only to find when she awoke that she would be connected to a horrendous breathing apparatus for the rest of her life. Knowing that she almost died during the surgery, this was not how she had envisioned her last years, so she chose to end her hard fight, knowing that her angels and God would be right around the corner.

I spent as much time as I could with my mother in her final days and visited our church several times, praying as hard as I could to the Virgin Mary for support. Mom herself had sought strength on many occasions from the Virgin Mother so I knew in my heart who I needed to pray to.

At one moment during her two-week fight for life, Mom told me the Virgin Mary had come to her and told her it was okay to let go. Mom said, "She was beautiful."

During her hospital stay, Mom scratched out several barely readable messages to us, as her way of communicating when she was conscious. One of her last handwritten messages to me was "keep the faith ... believe," which I have framed and it graces one of my office walls at home.

Over the years, Mom and I had long chats about a lot of things – family, work, politics, and what she called, and I now call, the "other side." She was a spiritual person who lived life to the fullest. I so loved our visits, especially when we talked about God, the angels, and what might lie ahead.

Mom and I had a pact, too. When she arrived on the "other side," she would let me know she was okay. We knew about the familiar phrase "pennies from heaven," so I would remind her to put a penny in my path from time to time, as a way to connect.

Just after Mom passed away, my sister and I left the hospital in separate cars. On my way home, I stopped at a convenience store to pick up the daily newspaper, and when I stepped out of my car there was a penny at my feet. I knew then that Mom hadn't wasted any time.

It was a long week of making funeral arrangements and saying final goodbyes. At the end of the week, after my mother's service, my husband Bruce and I retreated to the Berkshires, about 90 minutes from home, for a small respite.

It was during that trip, on June 14, 2008, that I experienced a spiritual awakening. Bruce and I had headed out for an early Saturday morning walk on a desolate road in Hancock, a hamlet in western Massachusetts. Just before we left, I had silently invited my mom to join us while we took in the majesty of Jiminy Peak.

The morning air was warm and breezy, ideal for the two-mile hike that Bruce and I decided we needed after our wrenching two weeks. As I walked, my heart was heavy with thoughts of Mom's passing. I had hoped that getting outdoors and enjoying the beauty of the Berkshires would take my mind off my sorrow. I didn't know that the dead-end road we were on would ultimately become my gateway to the afterlife. The evidence for it appeared later, in two photographs I took that morning – photographs that forever changed the way I look at the "other side."

Throughout my life, my mom and dad were always there for me with their love and support. I know that the love we shared on earth continues on in the spiritual realm. To this day, years after their passing, I look forward to seeing them again, either in a circular white light swirling around my home or in a photo I've taken.

My hope with this book is that those reading it will realize that they too are surrounded by angels and by their loved ones.

The walk in the Berkshires also opened my eyes to photography in a new and wonderful way. I hope my photos will inspire you to examine your own photographs for beautiful flashes of light: these are your loved ones and your guardian angels.

Whenever I am asked about my photos, I always maintain that we are never alone – our loved ones and guardian angels are close at hand. Their images, whether as pale circles, flashes of colorful light, or certain facial expressions in the clouds, remind us that those in the spirit realm want to connect with us.

During an angel reading in 2009, my guardian angels sent a message that inspired me to write this book. They told me, through Wendy, a gifted angel reader, not to be afraid but to tell the stories behind my photographs in hopes that they would help others heal.

I hope in some small way that seeing these photographs in which God's messengers appear will change your life, as they did mine.

One of my favorite photos is on the cover. My mom and dad are clearly watching over me from the "other side." When I was deciding which photo would best represent the book, this image came immediately to mind. I feel that it captures the essence of the book: angels are always by our side.

Now, whenever I take photos, I always keep a keen eye on the elements of the entire picture. Why? I don't want to miss a special visit from an angel.

Thank you for joining me on my spiritual journey. Godspeed.

Angel Encounters

My mom loved to talk about angels and would always remind me that angels protect us before it's our time to depart. However, until you experience your own angel encounter, it may seem difficult to grasp just how much power they have.

During the fall of 2009, within just two weeks, I was able to avoid two car accidents on busy roadways. I attribute my good fortune to guardian angels who intervened and took over my steering wheel.

In both cases, I never saw the cars speeding up behind me, but my angels did and acted to protect me. On both occasions, my steering wheel was taken over by a force that steered the car into a safer lane. Had the steering wheel not been manipulated, I could well have been killed by the impact of the speeding cars crashing into me from behind.

I've always believed in angels. But it took an angel reading – my first – to help me better understand them.

My friend Danielle and I had signed up for an evening of spiritual enlightenment in a Greek revival home in Westfield, Massachusetts. The clapboard house had been built originally for Merwin and Lydia Loomis in 1845, and its present owner had tastefully decorated it with antiques true to its historic period.

After an elegant meal, we made our way into the different areas of the house, meeting the presenters for the evening program. The house itself was a delight to see, with each well-appointed room offering a calm and serene space.

We chatted for about 10 minutes with each presenter, and Wendy, the angel reader, was among the presenters. She had established a warm and inviting atmosphere in a drawing room, where she laid out her angel cards on a tiny table. Her cards were bursting with color and featured different angels describing their roles as God's messengers.

As I passed by Wendy's tranquil space during the evening, I noticed that several women were drawing angel cards from the collection. Then, meeting Danielle halfway through the evening, I saw that she was filled with excitement after Wendy interpreted her cards. As a reporter, I am naturally curious, so I was intrigued by this and couldn't wait for my turn to select my own angel cards.

When the time came, I sat down with Wendy. The thought of a reading with my angels had never occurred to me before, but I felt open to a new experience. Wendy asked me if I talked to my angels on a regular basis. At first, I thought I had, but then I realized that I couldn't remember a time when I had actually had a real conversation with them.

Wendy put me at ease immediately. I thought I too would soon be drawing from her angel cards, but she said this wouldn't be necessary. She said my guardian angels were already communicating several messages to her, and they did not want the cards to hinder the communication.

Wendy said she saw me as a "lightworker," which she noted was a perfect complement to my love of photography and writing. She said that lightworkers are individuals incarnated specifically to help our world be a better place. Lightworkers have "a personal mission as well as a global mission," she said, to bring more love and light to the world.

She said my guardian angels urged her to relay to me the need to continue pursuing my photography because it would give others comfort.

"Pursue the gift you've been given," she said, noting that the angels would guide me in my pursuits; all I had to do was ask them. My angel reading ended with these instructions, said Wendy: "Don't be afraid – just do it."

Even though I had spent only 10 minutes with Wendy, being touched by my guardian angels in this way changed my life forever.

On that crisp fall Friday night, as leaves swirled and a light breeze caressed me, I said good night to Danielle and thanked her for joining me for an inspirational and life-changing evening. As I drove home, I realized how energized I felt, and I have since concentrated on the messages from my angels.

If any doubt lingered in my mind following that initial angel reading, it was put to rest four days later when I received a box of trinkets for an upcoming silent auction I was coordinating. Every year, a wonderful friend named Sue had contributed a variety of gifts that I used for a fall charity auction.

When I opened the box, I was stunned. There, lying beautifully on top of the donated auction items, were angels in all shapes and sizes. There were angel holiday ornaments, an angel necklace, an angel watch, and angel pins. I immediately emailed Sue to thank her and ask why she had included so many angels.

Astonished, she said she hadn't realized she had put the angels into the box. Later, she told me that when she heard my question, she felt goose bumps and was speechless. We agreed that our angels had coordinated their efforts to ensure that I would notice and take their messages to heart.

Since then, I have realized just how connected we are with our guardian angels. I now talk to my angels every day. I feel blessed to be in touch with them because this allows me in turn to reach out and touch others.

Don't ever hesitate to talk to your angels and ask for guidance. They are always close by, and I believe they want to comfort and aid us when we need them. Of course, I know in my heart that they also enjoy hearing us just say hello!

In the pages that follow, there are photographs that I believe clearly show how my guardian angels and loved ones let me know I am never alone.

Once you are in tune with the wonderful auras that can appear in photographs, I promise you that your pictures will take on an entirely new meaning.

The Journey Begins

These are the photographs of the Berkshire landscape where I began my spiritual awakening. This scene was awe-inspiring to me as a photographer when I first saw it, and it soon became even more remarkable when I discovered the flash of magenta light I couldn't explain amid the trees on the left. What I have since learned from that summer morning is that the aura of our guardian angels and our loved ones who have passed is always around us, watching over us, and can actually be captured on film.

June 2008, along Kittle Road in Hancock, MA. Jiminy Peak is in the background.

This photograph was taken about 20 minutes into our walk. I had invited my mom to join us on the trek, not realizing until I saw this photo that she was indeed with us. I did a double take when I first saw this photo, and after zooming in on the blue image on the left side, I saw my mom's face looking at me, forever changing the way I thought about the "other side." Thanks to this photograph, taken the day after my mom's funeral, I have no doubt that this was her way of saying "I made it fine!"

Together Again

As a fan of The Oprah Winfrey Show for many years, I had heard a lot about the writings of Eckhart Tolle and decided to bring his book, *A New Earth: Awakening to Your Life's Purpose*, with me on vacation to Bonaire a few weeks after the Berkshire visit.

Each afternoon I spent an hour or two on the beach, riveted by Tolle's message that one's inner purpose is to awaken. I was nearing the end of the book when I felt a shift in my being that I cannot describe or explain. I just knew instinctively that I had experienced an inner awakening.

As our Bonaire scuba diving vacation was coming to a close, Bruce and I traded the beach chairs for a day of kayaking alongside a picturesque mangrove forest. The time passed quickly on the water and I grew tired and realized how far away from the shore we actually were. As I struggled to continue paddling, I asked my dad for the strength and energy it would take to get back to shore. My dad had always been a pillar for me, from the height and stature he had inherited from his father to his well-worn hands that had toiled all his life in construction and manufacturing.

As you can see in this photo I took of Bruce several yards ahead of me, my dad's face comes through in a pink image with my mom's image in a white cloud just to the left of dad's face. A darkness in the sky brings the two images together.

Kayaking in Bonaire, July 2008.

Love is Eternal

The death of a loved one doesn't mean that the love that was shared has ended; but the grief of those left behind can be immeasurable.

My sister Bonnie has always had a deep faith. However, she has questioned that faith many times since losing her beloved husband Ian to cancer at age 52. It has now been more than 30 years since his passing, and as we chatted over lunch one day, I asked her if she wanted me to photograph her. She didn't hesitate – she said yes.

Bonnie works throughout the year in her spacious backyard, tending to every painstaking detail of her garden. I knew that her yard should be the setting for the photos.

After our lunch that summer afternoon, we drove to her home and I took 50 photographs of her. Of those 50, there was just one containing a special image. It was on the 11th picture.

When I called her later that evening, I told her about the photo with the beautiful white, heart-shaped light in it, and that it was the only one with such an image. She was startled when I said it was on the 11th photo. Ian had passed away on May 11.

My sister Bonnie in her backyard, Westfield, MA.

Traveling Companion

At first, my husband Bruce was skeptical about my thoughts on auras, so he purchased a new Canon camera to show me that there must have been issues with my original camera.

The angels, not missing a beat, decided to make a point in a picture he took with the new camera on a business trip to Delaware.

When he returned home from his trip, we noticed that the first photo he had taken had a beautiful white aura in it.

Bruce finally understood that our guardian angels were sending him a clear message. Since then, Bruce has carefully examined photos taken, looking forward to seeing the auras in our collective work.

A hotel room in Delaware.

Wishes Come True

My niece Donna has always had a strong faith. When she saw my photo of her mother with the white heart blazing in the background, she asked me to photograph her.

My sister Bonnie and I drove out one day to see Donna at her home in Connecticut. Donna is a nature lover, and at the time of our visit she was entertaining a squirrel named Zackary who stopped in every afternoon for some peanuts. In the photograph of this encounter, we saw a beautiful magenta aura watching over them just above the shed.

Donna was thrilled to have this photo and to know that her guardian angel was close by.

My niece Donna with Zackary in her backyard, Torrington, CT.

Flying High

As a reporter for a weekly family run newspaper for many years, I have had wonderful opportunities to cover stories and interview people I might not otherwise get to meet.

One fall day, I had the great pleasure of taking a trip with Pioneer Valley Balloons in Northampton, Massachusetts, led by owner and chief pilot Lisa Fusco.

As you can see by the photos, the magenta auras were not only flying high next to us, keeping a watchful eye, but were also floating right by our faces as we ascended into the early evening sky.

The author balloon-flying over Hampshire County with owner and chief pilot Lisa Fusco of Pioneer Valley Balloons in Northampton, MA.

Labyrinthine Journey

Labyrinths are one way to immerse oneself in the spirit world, according to Chaplain Therese J. Dube, a wonderful friend of mine.

Sister Therese is very open to the marvelous blessings we receive while on Mother Earth, and after looking through some of my photographs, we decided to photograph one of her labyrinth sessions.

A labyrinth, at its most basic level, is a model of the path that each one of us takes through life. The path allows us to journey to the center of our deepest selves and then back again, hopefully with a clearer understanding of who we are.

Sister Therese had lost her beloved mother and welcomed the chance to reconnect with her on a spiritual level. I took many photos of her while she was in the labyrinth, and several of them showed a white aura next to her.

Sister Therese loves this particular photo because the aura is in the cactus – keeping a watchful eye on the sanctity of the session.

When Sister Therese saw the photos, she said she was infused with a "quiet joy."

Chaplain Therese J. Dube, SAS V, MEd, MA, BCC, Veriditas-trained Labyrinth facilitator, conducts sessions with patients in Holyoke, MA.

We're Never Alone

Whether you are at home relaxing, getting ready to pack your bags for an adventure, or just going out to work, I believe that the loving spirits who are close to you will check on you often.

The key is not to become obsessed with connecting with the spirit world but to communicate when you need to really reach out and want to be touched.

I find that when I least expect it, my angels surprise me. And I've told my guardian angels and my mom and dad on numerous occasions that even when I'm well into my 90s, I'll still be looking for their auras in my photos.

The author at home during the holidays. A white aura rests on her right shoulder.

Bruce takes an early morning walk with our dog Ginger, as his guardian angel stays close.

Watchful Eyes

During the construction of our home, Bruce and I would check on each day's progress and always ask our dads to oversee the project from the "other side" while we were at work.

Bruce's dad had been a building contractor and my dad worked in construction for many years, so we knew that both of them would keep a keen eye on the construction crew.

During the foundation-pouring phase, we found a single penny glistening in the late afternoon sun, and we knew immediately that our dads had been watching. I had been on the lookout for a penny, knowing that it would be good luck to find one. Our dads didn't let us down.

What we didn't see initially, however, were the auras in the photos that were taken each day of the nine-month process. Months later, upon closer examination of the pictures, we did see the auras soaring over the construction site. They had been watching every detail of the project.

This is one of my favorite construction photos, where there is an aura nestled right next to my face. It was only after my own spiritual awakening that I actually saw the aura in this photo.

Family Affair

No one in my family likes to be reminded of another birthday, but that doesn't stop us from celebrating.

In the fall of 2009, my niece Donna and I surprised her mother with a birthday cake one warm Saturday afternoon.

As you can see, a beautiful aura joined us in the left side of the background.

My niece Donna cuts an ice cream cake for Bonnie, her mom, during a surprise birthday celebration.

Holiday Visitors

Auras can take many shapes, sizes, and colors, and on Christmas eve 2009, there were two that clearly wanted to be noticed by my camera lens.

Here, one aura is making a statement in the upper part of the photo by being at least twice the normal size of the auras that appear in my photos. A small spirit rests close to my niece on the couch on the right side of her shoulder.

Christmas Eve 2009 with my family. From left, Donna, Ian, Ian Michael, Ashley, and Laura.

Not Home Alone

Whether we're on a weekend getaway, or Bruce is working on a project in his workshop, we are reminded that our guardian angels and loved ones are close at hand in the beautiful auras that surround us.

Bruce puts the finishing touches on a workbench while several white auras oversee his progress.

On the author's fall hike up Jiminy Peak in Hancock, MA, a beautiful green aura joins the jaunt.

The author's puppy is unaware of sharing space with a beautiful aura on a camping trip.

Talking to Your Angels

Since my mom's passing, angels have opened my eyes – and my heart – to the glory of God. I am forever indebted to them for their love and support.

Whether I'm at home, at work, or on the road for a writing assignment, I know my angels can hear me and are always close by.

I take the time to talk to my angels every day, telling them I am thankful for their presence. I also confide in them and ask for their guidance when I need answers to questions or I'm seeking a healing presence.

As I've grown in my knowledge of my guardian angels, I find myself asking for their support more often. I know that they will be there for me, lovingly ready to help, no matter what my request. This is why I wrote this book.

My angels asked me to tell the stories surrounding my photos. They said through Wendy, the angel reader, "Book. Book. Book."

With all the blessings they have given me, I knew I couldn't let them down.

My hope with this book is to share my favorite photographs with you, and in the process, help you to pursue your own journey with the help of your guardian angels and those who have passed but are still close to you.

As I continue on my journey of discovery, I thank God and my guardian angels for giving me the ability to write this book.

Along the way, I had my doubts about whether I had what it would take to finish it. However, I had two experiences that solidified my belief that I could.

First, as I was asking for guidance and reassurance, there was one week during which I would periodically feel a surge in my being that I truly believe was the presence of the Holy Spirit. I will never forget those inner feelings that coursed through my body at the most unexpected moments. They came while I was at work and when I was home. I had never experienced them before – and haven't since.

Secondly, during a reporting assignment, I met a woman whose mother was clairvoyant. The woman emailed me the next day to tell me she had spoken with her mother about our time together, and her mother said she already knew all about me and about the book I was working on. I was stunned but also exhilarated, knowing these experiences were ways that God and my angels were telling me to persevere.

So I have followed the instructions of my guardian angels, to tell the stories behind my photos. I hope my pictures have opened up your heart and inspired you to take a second look at your own photos, or to take up the art of photography if you haven't before. It's as simple as picking up a camera and clicking the shutter.

I hope you will find peace, joy, and an inner strength from these pages. What I learned early on in my angel readings was to be positive, patient, and open to all the possible messages sent by the powerful angels who share our life experiences with us.

It is my hope that you will see the beautiful bands and areas of color – what I personally consider an angel's presence – in your photos. You should also go back to old photos you've taken to see if an angel appears in them. I did this myself with photos taken during earlier family occasions and found auras that I had previously missed.

I believe our heavenly helpers are always nearby, ready to assist us through their divine intervention, as well as to help promote God's plans for us.

In my heart I am convinced that God shelters me with angels who will see me through both good and trying times until my own "time" arrives to be welcomed home. Scripture tells us there is a time to be born and a time to die. When my time arrives to pass, I will welcome my angels with open arms, and I know they will comfort me and bring me peace. Of course, I know my mom and dad will be the next in line to say hello.

From my angel readings I learned I have two guardian angels. Each night before I go to sleep, I ask them for a restful night's slumber. One morning, my sleep ended with the most wonderful wake-up call.

It was a workday morning and soon the alarm would be sounding off. What awakened me this particular morning was not the alarm but the sounds of giggling in my left ear. The beautiful sounds were sweet, playful, and childlike – sounds I will always treasure – and I immediately thanked my angels for allowing me into their world for a few seconds. The giggling in my ear, on April 15, 2010, has remained a treasured moment in time.

I've also learned through angel readings that our loved ones want to connect with us while we're asleep, and on several occasions my mom and dad have done this for me.

One year after my mom's passing, I knew that I wanted to try connecting with her on a different level, and asked her to help me find a way to do this. I had missed her so much. Then one very early morning, I dreamt I was transporting Mom in a car and she desperately needed to quench her thirst. I stopped the car and assisted her with some water, and as she finished, she put her arms lovingly around me. At that moment, I felt the most intense warmth rush through my body, which I know was her way of expressing her love for me. That too was a feeling I will remember and always treasure.

I now keep a pen and journal on my bedside table so I can jot down experiences, key words and phrases, and conversations from my dreams while they are fresh in my mind. I refer to my journal often and treasure the wonderful memories it holds.

Taking Aim At Photography

Although I take photographs every day, I don't always see special images or auras. My angels explained to me through angel readings that they arrive when I need a message, or perhaps when I need to be reassured about a decision I am contemplating, or when I need to feel comforted.

"They show when they need to" was the direct message from one of my angel readings.

Also, during a reading, my angels told me that this book would be a "realizing point" in my journey. My journey would continue to evolve and I needed to "let it happen," they said. As I follow my angels' advice and let this wonderful experience unfold, I know I will be guided by the beautiful light that surrounds me.

What I know for certain is that angels are all around us.

Final Thoughts

Cynics will suggest that my camera had flaws, that perhaps there was a problem with the lenses or camera body that affected the photos I've shared with you.

Since the summer of 2008, I have had four Canon digital cameras, and the beautiful auras have appeared in photos from every one of them.

So to any who may dismiss me and this book, I say those who don't believe are missing out on a wonderful existence here on Mother Earth.

This may be one of the lessons the skeptics need to learn while they are here – before they too are "called home."

Thank you for sharing my spiritual journey with me.

I hope that you will experience the enlightenment that is open to all of us, simply by asking your guardian angels for guidance.

Your Life's Journey

The stage is now set. It is up to you to take the next step.

Are you ready? Are you open to the wondrous ways your guardian angels will be connecting with you in the months and years to come? Do you trust in your guardian angels to open up a new world for you?

I hope you do. Once you make your first connection, I promise that your life will be changed forever.

Please remember that patience is the key to any new practice, and with it will come a new, profound appreciation for what God offers us on earth and in our continuing journey through life everlasting.

Try also to remember it will take diligence, patience, and time for you to connect with your spirit family. I believe that because they too want to connect with you, you become part of a partnership based on mutual love that transcends time and space.

Enjoy your newfound knowledge. It opens a door to a new way of thinking – and, in the process, opens your heart to more loving and positive thoughts.

The sky is your limit, so don't waste another minute. Pick up a camera, start shooting, and discover the wonders that surround you.

God bless!

Printed in the United States
by Baker & Taylor Publisher Services